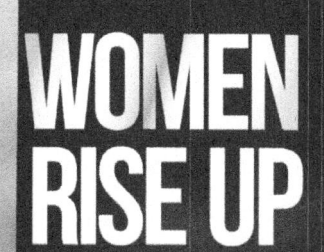

WOMEN RISE UP
AND CRY OUT FOR THE DESTINIES OF YOUR CHILDREN

Helen Wialo Chongsi

Women Rise Up and Cry Out for the Destinies of Your Children

Copyright © January 2025
Helen Chongsi
All rights reserved!

ISBN: 978-1-63603-297-9

Published by
IEM Press
A Subsidiary of IEM Approach LLC.
Richardson, Texas, USA.

For more information, please write to:
Mrs. Helen Wialo Chongsi
513 Brinwood Way
Oakley, CA 94561-3089
Email: helenchongsi11@gmail.com
Phone: (+1) 925-567-4167

(+237) 696-524-859
(+237) 677-21-97-22

IEM PRESS are honored to present this title with the author. The views expressed or implied in this work are those of the author. IEM Press provides our imprint seal representing design excellence, creative content and high-quality production. To learn more about IEM Press visit www.iempublishing.com or reach us via iempress2016@gmail.com or +237 672-82-77-84

No part of this publication may be reproduced, stored in a retrieval system, or transmitted in any form or by any means, including electronic, photocopy, or recording, without the prior written permission of the publisher.

Women Rise Up and Cry for the Destinies of Your Children

Dedication

To my dear teacher, the Holy Spirit, who led me and taught me to write this book.

Acknowledgments

I want to give a vote of thanks to my dear brother and sister, Rev. Pastor John and Patti Brown, who stood by me and encouraged me to write this manuscript.

I am grateful to our Patron, Pastor Darryl Walker, the only man who has stood by us from 2018 until today, and to his wife, Karen Walker, who assisted me in leading.

I am also grateful to my lovely Friday night prayer warriors, who took the time to pray for me while I was writing.

A big "thank you" to my Pastor and wife, Vance and Laura Murphy, who cared for me both spiritually and materially at the ARC.

I also thank my former Pastor, Rev. Godson Nembo Tangumonkem, in Bamenda, Cameroon, who taught us to pray as a church, both by praying himself and by taking us to different prayer mountains.

I am immensely grateful to my children, Rev. Godswill and Mrs. Florence Chongsi, Mr. and Mrs. Neuafonkom, and Patience, who stood by me to get this book typed and translated into French.

I sincerely appreciate the efforts of Pastor Chaplain Emmanuel Tangumonkem and his team in ensuring that this book is well-crafted and released to the masses.

Endorsements

"This book is an urgent call to action. In its pages, Mama Helen Chongsi invites Christian women to arise and take their place in God's agenda for their lives. She urges them to awaken to the divine mandate God has bestowed upon them and function in that mandate unapologetically. For Christian mothers, this mandate translates into fervent, profound, relentless, and compelling prayers to enact God's destiny in the lives of their children, families, and the community at large.

I strongly recommend this book to women, especially mothers, who feel that they have been kept on the back burner unduly, relegated into inertia for too long, and wish, through heartfelt prayers, to bring into manifestation the divine program that has been dormant in their lives."

Emmanuel Oumarou, *Ph.D. (Miss); Ph.D. (Theo. & ICS); CertMed.*
Director of Theological Institute for Missions and Intercultural Studies (TIMIS), Bamenda, Cameroon.

"I met Helen in 2006 when she came to the church my family and I attended in Douglasville, GA. That meeting (as I would later discover and learn), was God-ordained. The Holy Spirit of God the Father and God the Son was at work, answering the cry in my heart for God to provide a discipler I could meet with regularly. He answered that prayer and in my wildest of dreams I couldn't have imagined she would come, all the way from Africa, and show

up on the very day that I was ready to go on a run with discouragement in my heart having no particular person to fellowship with.

I learned by way of the Holy Spirit that Helen carried the spirit of intercession and the time had come for her to release it to the gathering of people who gave themselves to prayer. For two years, simply by "showing up," I witnessed movement and came to believe that the Lord's heart for His people is revealed in prayer, with power released through intercession. Helen released that over us in a prayer group (8-12 people) that started meeting as we met on Friday nights from midnight to 3 am. The gift of God's heart and the power of praying in tongues filled our gatherings, compelling us to intercede and allowing His power to overflow into our families and circumstances.

I learned that God works according to His measure and timing, He uses servants like

Helen—who I see as someone who carries a burden to awaken intercessors in the city of Atlanta. They are gifts given from above, showing us in tangible ways what it means to be a living sacrifice, holy and pleasing to the Lord (Romans 12:1-2). My sister Helen embodied this and graciously brought it to us both in her presence and now in a small book format.

I am convinced that the contents of this book reflect God's heart for His church. Intercessors are being birthed and ignited by His holy fire through the thoughts and testimonies it contains.

Humbly, I come and testify,"

Evelyn Huth
USA

"*Mama, as we often call her, is somebody who easily carries the burden as children are concerned irrespective of the family, the tribe, or the nation a child is from. As a wailing woman, a member of a group called Wailing Women Worldwide, and as one of the pioneer coordinators in the North West region of Cameroon, she has what it takes to convince people to pray for a change as negative situations appear. Each time we went out to raise Wailing Women, she was usually the one who emphasized the importance of prayer to the women. I recommend this book to every woman who wants to see what God can do to change children, even the ones we think are very very bad."*

Anne Kamdem

North West Regional Coordinator of the Wailing Women in Cameroon

"A compelling call to action! Mother Helen rallies the mothers of this generation to contend for the destinies of their families and children *through prayer. Hope-inspiring and power-packed, this book is a 'must-read!'"*

Karen T. Walker
Director of The Way Training Center for Women
421 E. 15th St., Atlanta, USA

"I have had the pleasure of knowing Mama Helen Chongsi for almost two decades, dating back to her time with us at Full Gospel Mission Cow Street in Bamenda, Cameroon. She has continuously inspired me with her unwavering faith and fervent prayers as a dedicated intercessor. Her commitment to seeking God's will and interceding for others is truly commendable. Through my experiences with her, I have learned that God works according to His own measure and timing. He uses servants like Mama Chongsi—who carries a burden to awaken intercessors wherever she goes. They are gifts from above, demonstrating in tangible ways what it

means to be a living sacrifice, holy and pleasing to the Lord (Romans 12:1-2).

"Women Rise Up and Cry Out for the Destinies of Your Children" is a powerful call to action. Mama Chongsi encourages mothers of this generation to contend for the destinies of their children, families, and communities through prayer. This book is an invaluable resource that offers practical guidance on how to engage in effective prayer and intercession. It is both inspiring and empowering—a true must-read! I wholeheartedly endorse this book to all women who wish to deepen their spiritual lives and positively impact the world."

Emmanuel Nembundah Tangumonkem
*Pastor/Chaplain,
National Youth Secretary,
Full Gospel Mission Cameroon
V.P., Cameroon Chaplains Association*

WOMEN RISE UP AND CRY FOR THE DESTINIES OF YOUR CHILDREN

Table of Contents

DEDICATION V

ACKNOWLEDGMENTS VII

ENDORSEMENTS.. IX

HOW TO BECOME A CHILD OF GOD XXI

INTRODUCTION.. 31

CHAPTER ONE: WOMEN ON ANSWER 37

    AN ASSIGNMENT FROM THE LORD ... 38

    THE LORD CAN DECIDE TO TURN AWAY HIS ANGER WHEN HIS PEOPLE CRY 48

WOMEN, YOU ARE PREGNANT WITH DELIVERERS, PROPHETS, MISSIONARIES, PRESIDENTS, ETC!.. 53

Chapter Two: REFUSE TO TAKE NO, FOR AN ANSWER 63

FIRST BIBLICAL EXAMPLE: HANNAH 63

THE SECOND BIBLICAL EXAMPLE: THE WOMAN OF CANAAN 70

THE THIRD BIBLICAL EXAMPLE: THE WOMAN WITH THE ISSUE OF BLOOD... 76

THE FOURTH BIBLICAL EXAMPLE: MARY MAGDALENE.......................... 80

Chapter Three: A WOMAN IS A VESSEL IN THE HANDS OF THE LORD 91

THE FIRST EXAMPLE: VIRGIN MARY . 91

THE SECOND EXAMPLE: DEBORAH... 93

THE THIRD EXAMPLE: ANNA THE WIDOW 94

THE FOURTH EXAMPLE: QUEEN ESTHER 96

WHAT FASTING AND PRAYERS CAN DO 99

CHAPTER FOUR: PRAYER IS HARD WORK 115

NEHEMIAH REBUILDS THE BROKEN WALL 115

DAVID BEFORE GOLIATH 118

IS YOUR CASE LIKE THE DRY BONES? 120

THIS IS YOUR GENERATION! 122

PRAYER IS WORK! 123

CALLED TO STAND IN THE GAP FOR YOUR FAMILIES 125

THE BLOOD OF JESUS SPEAKS BETTER THINGS 127

GO FOR ANOINTING!..........................131

CONCLUSION... 137

How to Become a Child of God

Going to church and praying is not enough. *"Except a man is BORN AGAIN, he CANNOT SEE the kingdom of God." (John 3:3).*
The following steps will help you know how you can be born again.

Step 1: God Loves You and Offers a Wonderful Plan for Your Life

"For God so loved the world that He gave His only begotten Son, that whoever believes in Him should not perish but have everlasting life" (John 3:16). Jesus said, *"I came that they*

might have life and have it to the full." (John 10:10).

No matter who you are and what you have done, God still loves you and wants to save you (Rom.5:8).

Step 2: Your Sins Have Separated You from God; That Is Why You Are Not Experiencing His Wonderful Plan for Your Life

"For all have sinned and fall short of the glory of God" (Rom.3:23) "The wages of sin is death (spiritual separation from God) Rom.6:23. All your religious activities and efforts cannot save you. God has provided a solution for you.

Step 3: Jesus Christ Is the Only Way Back to God

Jesus said, *"I am the way, the truth and the life, No one comes to the father except through me" (John 14:6).* Jesus is the only sacrifice God can accept for your sins. Through Him you can connect to God's plan for your life.

Step 4: You Must Personally Receive Jesus Christ as Your Saviour and Lord. Then You Can Know and Experience God's Plan for Your Life

Receive Him by personal invitation and by faith. *"Behold, I stand at the door and knock. If anyone hears My voice and opens the door (your heart), I will come in to him and dine with him, and he with Me." (Rev.3:20).*

If you are ready now to give your life to Jesus Christ, pray this prayer with all your heart.

"Dear Lord Jesus Christ, I need you. I open the door of my life and receive you as my Saviour and Lord. Forgive all my sins and wash me with your blood. Make me the kind of person you want me to be. Thank you for saving me."

Congrats! You are now a child of God.

Making the decision to become a born-again Christian, is the best decision you've ever made in your entire life and I congratulate you for that. The following points will help you enjoy your newfound life in Christ Jesus.

1. **Live with the Consciousness that You are Saved:** It is fundamental that you are certain of your new faith. This is referred to as the Assurance of Salvation. Believe that your sins have been forgiven and forgotten by God because of the price Jesus paid by His sacrificial death on the cross and that you are no longer under any condemnation (Acts 16:31, Rom.8:1-2, 2Cor.5:17, Jn.1:12).

2. **Join a Fellowship:** By new birth, you have entered the family of God. Locate a church that teaches and practises the scriptures truthfully, where the worship enables you to encounter God, and where the people are friendly and

spiritual growth is encouraged (Heb.10:25, Gal.6:10).

3. **Get a Bible and Study It Daily:** You can begin from John, then Acts, Romans, etc. Just as a baby needs physical nourishment in order to grow, the Word of God is also the spiritual food by which we grow into Christlikeness (1Pet.2:2, Jn.5:24). Consult other mature Christians for any explanations.

4. **Commune Daily with God:** Through prayer, we talk with God, express our burdens to Him, as well as offer worship, praise and appreciation. We also have the privilege to get God speak to us, showering upon us His love,

peace, blessings and divine direction (Rom.10:9, 1Thess.5:17, 1Pet.5:8).

5. **Destroy Satan's Property in Your Keeping:** Desist from anything that does not glorify God. Do away with anything evil related to your sinful past, such as pornographic materials, stolen money and possessions, talismans, charms, juju, etc. (2Cor.6:17, Tit.2:11).

6. **Separate from Evil Friends and Get New Godly Friends:** Now that you are born again, you must discontinue the former way of life and walk in the truth (Ps.1:1-3, 2Cor.4:2; 5:17, Eph.4:22, 1Jn.1:6).

7. **Get Baptized:** Water baptism by immersion publicly authenticates our salvation and affirms our membership in the body of Christ (Rom.6:4, Col.2:12, Matt.28:19, Acts 2:38, 8:36).

8. **Seek the Baptism of the Holy Spirit:** The Holy Spirit assures us that we are saved and empowers us to live a holy life and do exploits for God through special gifts (Rom.8:14, Acts 2:1-4; 10:38, Eph.5:18).

9. **Tell Others about Jesus:** Our character should testify about our inner transformation. Also, our eagerness to tell others about God's love and lead them to Christ is also evidential about

our salvation (Jn.4:28-29, Acts 4:10; 22:14, 2Tim.2:2).

10. **Worship God with Your Wealth through Offerings and Tithes:** Our cheerful giving is essential in advancing God's Kingdom – freewill offerings and tithe (one-tenth of our increase) (Deut.16:16-17, Prov.3:9-10, 2Cor:9:7).

11. **Make the Life of Christ Your Standard:** Fix your eyes on Jesus, the Author and Finisher of our faith Make Him your Role Model (Heb.12:2, Phil.2:5-11, Eph.4:24).

12. **Don't Abandon; Rise and Continue, if you Fall:** The Christian race may seem

tough and challenging, with persecutions, distractions, opposition, and even discouragements. But rest assured, you will make it by faith (Prov.24:16, Isa.41:10, Phil.1:6).

I pray that you will stand firm, and finish well like other heroes of faith, in Jesus' name! Amen.

Call us for counselling and prayer: (+1) 925-567-4167 or (+237) 679-46-57-17.

Introduction

On April 6, 2018, we established an intercessory prayer group at the ARC – Atlanta Revival Center in Atlanta, Georgia. We met every Friday night from 10 pm to 2 am. As we began to pray, we witnessed the Hand of the Lord at work! We prayed for one of our children who was scheduled for surgery, and through prayer, the Lord intervened in that situation. We also prayed for several children who had been kidnapped; by

God's grace, the kidnappers were exposed, and the children were safely released.

One of the intercessors brought forth a request to pray for a couple who wanted to transition their only male child into a female. As we prayed, the couple took their son for surgery, but the state where the procedure was to occur requested that they relocate from their current residence. When they prepared to leave, the husband lost his job. While we continued to pray, the COVID-19 outbreak began. Eventually, the boy realized that he identified as male and chose to leave his parents to live with a relative, thereby sparing his life. We thank the Lord who spared his life through prayers.

Some individuals requested prayer for young children aged 11 to 12 years who had expressed a desire to change their genders. My heart broke, and I cried out to the Lord, questioning how a 12-year-old girl could boldly tell her parents that she wanted to be a boy. I wondered where they got such ideas. I believe the Holy Spirit revealed to me that the enemy is targeting our younger generations—our children and grandchildren. Many parents, however, do not see the potential harm in a child wanting to change their gender.

The Holy Spirit inspired me to write this book especially for women. It aims to empower them to travail, wail, rise up, and cry out for the destinies of our children, who are under threat. I believe that the

Lord is counting on women because they possess the perseverance needed for prayer. This little book is a prayer guide to help you pray as you read along. It is not a history book!

HOW TO PRAY WITH THIS LITTLE PRAYER GUIDE

1) Read the scriptures attached to every prayer topic well, and use the word of God in the scriptures to pray the topics.
2) You can use this guide to raise an Altar of prayer for your family,
Church, and the Nation.

REPENTANCE!

Before we begin to pray, let us ask the Lord to forgive us for the following:

1) Being nonchalant; as mentioned in Revelation 3:15-16, 18.
2) As mothers, we may not have taken the time to listen to our children, to fellowship with them, or to allow them to express their thoughts. Because of this, we may provoke them to anger (Colossians 3:21). "I acknowledge that I have been guilty of this many times. Father, forgive me!"

Chapter One

WOMEN ON ASSIGNMENT

The Lord is calling on women—mothers—to rise and pray for the destinies of their children and grandchildren. Woman, you are a mother! Whether or not you have biological children, you embody the spirit of motherhood. This little book in your hands serves as a prayer guide to assist you. You may have read many books on prayer, but now is the time to engage in prayer, and this little guide will help you do just that.

AN ASSIGNMENT FROM THE LORD

"And there followed him a great company of people, and women, which also bewailed and lamented him. But Jesus turning unto them said, 'daughters of Jerusalem, weep not for me, but weep for yourselves, and for your children. For, behold, the days are coming, in which they shall say: 'blessed are the barren, and the wombs that never bare, and the paps which never gave suck.'" (Luke 23:27-29)

From the Garden of Gethsemane, where the Lord's sweat was like drops of blood, He endured pain at the hands of those to whom He had willingly surrendered Himself for crucifixion. Finally, He arrived at a place where the crowd from Jerusalem followed Him, wailing. At this moment, He was just minutes away from paying the ultimate price for humanity's redemption, to bring humankind back to God. What a time of darkness and pain it was for the Lord! Yet, He turned to the daughters of Jerusalem and instructed them not to weep for Him, but to weep for themselves and their children, regarding the troubles that were to come in the days ahead. This scripture is being fulfilled right before our eyes.

Mothers, this warning is for you and me today! In the Scripture above, the Lord Jesus refers to the destruction of Jerusalem. However, if He were here today, what else do you think He would say to us about our children? When the Bible talks of the daughters of Jerusalem, it refers to men and women alike. Look around you and see the orphans, the castaways, the homeless, those who are being kidnapped and taken to unknown destinations, and victims of human trafficking. The command from the Lord is that we should cry for ourselves and our children. The enemy has buried their destinies in drugs; the unborn are killed, amongst other social ills. It is time to cry; it is time to mourn, to wail for the destinies of children.

Women, do you know that you can arise in the middle of the night and use the rod, which is your tongue, to point to the East, to the West, to the North, and the South, and prophesy to that baby in the womb of a woman whom you do not you know; to arise, and fight the abortionist who is standing out there to take him out? You may not believe it, but try it. Your tears and your tongue have power! Mother/Intercessor, you do not need to fly to any part of the world before you prophesy; do it right where you are.

> *"The Earth is the Lord's, and the fulness thereof, the World and they that dwell therein." (Psalm 24:1)*

I am from Africa, and I have seen children who had been abandoned on the wayside by young girls, who were picked up by Christian mothers just like you, who took care of them physically and spiritually and they are fulfilling their destinies today. From verse 29 of Luke chapter 23, one can tell that those evil days are already here; it is happening all over the world. Mothers, does it mean anything to you that a son who was born into a family, is bold enough at the age of 10-12 to tell his parents that he wants to be a girl? Girls on the other hand want to be boys. Christian women, are you still sleeping??? Cry out to the Lord; "FATHER, WAKE US FROM SLUMBER!!!"

Thomas Andrew (1873-1912) was born like any other child and grew up alongside other children. His mother may not have known who he would become, just as you and I cannot predict the future. Before reaching the age of 39, he became a shipbuilder, and the last ship he built was the ocean liner known as the Titanic. The ship was constructed so meticulously that its captain, Edward John Smith, boastfully declared, "Even God Himself couldn't sink this ship." Thomas was equally confident, reportedly telling a friend that the Titanic was "as nearly perfect as human brains can make her." Tragically, on April 15, 1912, this young and talented man was among the more than 1,500 individuals who perished when the ship sank, despite being believed unsinkable—even by God. He was only 39 years old. One wonders if he had someone to caution him about such arrogance. Remember, the Lord has given you wisdom to accomplish whatever you set out to do; give Him glory! Christian mothers, we have a responsibility to guide all children to the Lord, not just our biological children. Your prayers can truly make a difference, even for a child across the world. Don't hesitate to lovingly correct those around you, wherever you may be. We will all stand before our Lord and Savior, Jesus Christ, one day.

As I mentioned earlier, the little book you are holding is a prayer guide, and you can read it and pray at the same time. Time does not wait for anyone, sisters! In Acts 23:12–16, we learn about around 40 individuals who vowed to abstain from food and drink until they had killed the Apostle Paul. Could you imagine the enemy could fast? But the Lord intervened. Beloved sisters, as you can see on your phones, the enemy is constantly attempting to come up with new ways to capture the minds of our children. Demonic spirits are trying to influence their minds and change their identities. Let us shout in gratitude: "O Lord, thank you, for being the Way, the Truth, and the Life!" "Thank You for paying for our redemption, and the redemption of our descendants with Your Precious Blood." You can add your topics and continue to pray. Remember that this is a prayer guide. As you can see, the adversary is training the children to reject and alter God's exquisite handiwork in their lives. As young as our children are, can you image the evil the enemy is instilling in their thoughts at their tender ages, to have the audacity to tell the Lord, "I want to change who You created me to be." Mothers, let us cry to the Lord for mercy on our children.

As I move around the neighborhood, I see some of these young kids and I believe you also see them, singing in their little groups; some playing football made of rags. This happens mostly in Africa. Some of them practice what they learn from Sunday School and the Church. I begin to imagine their destinies; some will be presidents, missionaries, pastors, teachers, real estate agents, housewives, fathers, and mothers. Then I hear the Holy Spirit ministering to me: "How are the above going to be fulfilled?" The enemy who failed to kill them from the womb is still looking for a way to derail their lives. The Lord's command to cry is urgent!!!

> *Lamentations 2:19. "Arise, cry out in the night: In the beginning of the watches pour out your heart like water before the face of The Lord: lift up thy hands towards Him for the lives of your young children that faint for hunger in top of every street."*

The hunger in the verse above may not be for food; it could be the hunger for the truth they need to know, which will set them free (John 8:32).

> *Proverbs 22:6 "Train up a child in the way he should go; and when he is old he will not depart from it."*

In Psalm 126:5-6, The Bible says,

> *"They that sow in tears shall reap in joy. He that goth forth, and weepeth, bearing precious seed, shall doubtless come again with rejoicing, bringing in his sheaves with him."*

THE LORD CAN DECIDE TO TURN AWAY HIS ANGER WHEN HIS PEOPLE CRY

According to Jeremiah 8:1-22, Israel, the chosen Nation of the Lord, sinned against Him; they rejected the Word of the Lord.

> *Verse 10: "Therefore I will give their wives unto others, and their fields to them that shall inherit them: for everyone from the least even unto the greatest is given to covetousness,*

from the prophet even unto the priest every one dealeth falsely."

Verse 13: "I will surely consume them, saith the Lord: there shall be no grapes on their vine, nor figs on the fig tree, and the leaf shall fade; and the things that I have given them shall pass away from them."

Tears are a strong prayer language!

Tears are a prayer language the Lord understands and easily accessible to women. Men may try, but they cannot beat the women. Jeremiah the prophet thought he could handle the situation, as we see in Jeremiah 9:1-2.

Verse 10: "He said; 'I will take up a weeping, and wailing for the

> *mountains, and for the dwelling places of the wilderness a lamentation, because are burned up"'.*

The Lord saw that he was eager to plead for forgiveness for his nation and cause the Lord to change His mind concerning the land, but instead sent him to the women.

> *"Thou says The Lord of Hosts; consider and call for the mourning women, that they come; and send for the skillful wailing women that they may come. Let them make haste and take up a wailing for us, that our eyes may run with tears, and our eyelids gush with water." (Jeremiah 9:17-19).*

Jeremiah went straight to call for the mourning, wailing women to come alongside their daughters, as the Lord instructed him.

Verse 20: "Yet hear the word of The Lord, O women, and let your ear receive the word of His mouth; teach your daughters wailing, and everyone her neighbor a lamentation".

When the wailing women came together to release the kind of prayers through tears that are understood only by the Lord, He changed His mind concerning the judgment that was to come upon Israel.

Tears are another dimension of prayer that come from a desperate heart!

If Prophet Jeremiah was able to retreat into the wilderness and weep for his people's transgressions, how much more can we today? The ship appears to be doing well, but it is actually sinking. In these perilous days, may women rise up and cry out for the family, the church, and the nation.

Mothers, be violent! Mathew 11:12. The above topics are meant to assist you; instead of just reading them, you should spend time to pray them. You can focus on one issue for ten minutes.

Make sure you add your own topics. Be determined! Declare what you want to see in the lives of your children.

> *"Dear Holy Spirit, my Teacher, Comforter, and Helper, we cannot do without You. Please teach us how to pray and how to sow the precious seeds of*

Your word into the hearts of our descendants."

WOMEN, YOU ARE PREGNANT WITH DELIVERERS, PROPHETS, MISSIONARIES, PRESIDENTS, ETC!

Moses, whom the Lord used to deliver the children of Israel from Egypt, was born at a time when Pharaoh issued a command detailed in Exodus 1:22:

"And Pharaoh charged all his people, saying, 'Every son that is born you shall cast into the river, and every daughter you shall save alive.'"

Exodus 2:1-2: "And there went a man of the house of Levi, and took to wife a daughter of Levi. And the woman conceived, and bare a son: and when she saw him that he was a goodly child, hid him three months. For three months Moses's mom prayed for him in hiding, after that she took him, and placed him by the river brink in Egypt."

It is reasonable to believe that even after leaving him by the river, Jochebed, Moses' mother continued to pray for her baby. This is likely why she found favor with the Lord and was chosen to nurse him. At this point, she had the opportunity to pray over him and teach Moses. There is a communication between a mother and her baby that only the Lord understands. Even while in the womb, a baby can comprehend their mother's voice. I can imagine Moses's mother telling him, "Look, you are an

Israelite, not an Egyptian." As mothers, we have the responsibility to teach our children about their identity and to let them know that God had a purpose for them even before they were formed in the womb, as stated in Jeremiah 1:5:

> *"Before I formed thee in the belly, I knew thee; and before thou cometh forth out of the womb, I sanctified thee and ordained thee a prophet unto the nations."*

Please pray as you read on; this serves as a prayer guide, not merely a history book. Many of us are what we are today because of the prayers of our grandparents, parents, and others. Rise up and pray for your children—the storms of evil are threatening their lives. Lay your hands on them as they sleep and command the works of the enemy to be broken off their lives. As stated in Lamentations 3:37,

> *"Who is he that says, and it comes to pass, when the Lord commanded it not?"*

Pray that every negative word spoken by the enemy against your children be annulled by the Blood of Jesus. Ezekiel 22:30 tells us,

> *"And I sought for a man among them, that should make up the hedge and stand in the gap before Me for the land that I should not destroy it: but I found none."*

In this verse, the Lord was looking for someone to stand in the gap for Jerusalem, which had been corrupted by the shedding of innocent blood by Manasseh. Even though this evil warranted judgment, the Lord still sought one man or woman to stay His hand of judgment, but found none. He is a merciful Father and will not destroy your family without warning.

Christian mothers and intercessors, the Lord is counting on you. You have the ability to change the course of your family, church, community, and nation.

Prayer Topics

1. *Dear Father, thank You for Your love for me; it is the reason this prayer guide is in my hands.*
2. *Thanksgiving unto You Lord, for Your loving-kindness that endures forever. Psalm 118:1.*

3. *Father, I thank You for the gift of children.*
4. *Thank You Lord for giving us women the ability to stand in the gap for the children and grandchildren. Ezekiel 22:30.*
5. *Dear Lord, give us the grace to raise the children according to Your Word. Proverbs 22:6.*
6. *Let the Blood of Jesus speak deliverance, complete healing from every entanglement, freedom, victory and blessings. Let open doors be granted to the children in the mighty name of Jesus.*
7. *Any command of "make sure" working against the lives of my children and grandchildren, let the earth quake, and break it in the Mighty Name of Jesus. Matthew 27:64-66.*

8. *I silence the voice of the enemy that is speaking against my children when the Lord has not commanded: Lamentations 3:37.*
9. *I decree and declare that I and my children and my grandchildren shall do signs and wonders in the mighty name of Jesus. Isaiah 8:18. They will fulfill their purpose of creation in the Mighty Name of Jesus. Jeremiah 1:5.*
10. *O Lord, arise and contend with the enemies that are contending with our children. Isaiah 49:24-26.*
11. *Arise O Lord, and let the enemies that have tried to derail the destinies of the children be scattered, in the Mighty Name of Jesus! Numbers 10:35.*
12. *Holy One of Israel, let every network of the enemy against our children and grand-*

children be broken into pieces and their counsel be brought to naught, in the Mighty Name of Jesus. Isaiah 8:9-10.

13. *Dear Lord, we stand on the authority that You have given us through the Blood of Jesus to declare war against the evil spirit, ancestral spirit from the pit of hell, assigned to destroy the destinies of the young children, in the Mighty Name of Jesus. Isaiah 54:15, 17.*

14. *O Lord!, let Your terror visit the enemy camp that has caged and held the destinies of our children and grandchildren in captivity, in the Mighty Name of Jesus. 2 Kings 7:3-7.*

15. *I declare that my children will thrive in faith, show kindness to others, and grow in*

wisdom. May they follow Your guidance and be filled with love and joy in their lives."

16. *Father, I thank You because my descendants and I will fulfill the purpose of our creation. Isaiah 8:18.*

Add your own topics and please spend time in prayer!

Stand in the gap and remain steadfast! It's not a one-day journey. The enemy does not go on vacation (1 Peter 5:8).

Women Rise Up and Cry for the Destinies of Your Children

CHAPTER TWO

REFUSE TO TAKE NO, FOR AN ANSWER

THE FIRST BIBLICAL EXAMPLE: HANNAH
(1 Samuel 1:1-18)

Now there was a certain man of Ramathaim-Zophim, of Mount Ephraim, and his name was Elkanah, the son of Jeroham, the son of Elihu, the son of Tohu, the son of Zuph, an Ephrathite. He had two wives: the name of one was Hannah, and the name of the other was Peninnah. Peninnah had children, but Hannah had no children. This man went up out of his city yearly to worship and to sacrifice to the Lord of Hosts at Shiloh. When it was time for Elkanah to offer, he gave to Peninnah his wife and to all her sons and daughters portions; but unto Hannah he gave a worthy portion, for he loved Hannah, but the Lord had shut up her womb. Her adversary provoked her sorely to make her fret or worry, because the Lord had shut up her womb.

Year after year, when she went up to the house of the Lord, she was provoked; therefore, she wept and did not eat. Then Elkanah, her husband, said to her, 'Hannah, why are you weeping? Why don't you eat? Why is your heart grieved? Am I not better to you than ten sons?' So Hannah rose up after they had eaten in Shiloh and after they had drunk. Now Eli the priest sat upon a seat by a post of the temple of the Lord. She was in bitterness of soul and prayed to the Lord, weeping sorely. She vowed a vow and said, 'O Lord of Hosts, if You will indeed look on the affliction of Your handmaid and remember me, and not forget Your handmaid, but will give Your handmaid a man child, then I will give him to the Lord all the days of his life, and there shall no razor come upon his head.'

As she continued praying before the Lord, Eli marked her mouth. Now Hannah spoke in her heart; only her lips moved, but her voice was not heard. Therefore, Eli thought she had been drunk. Eli said to her, 'How long will you be drunk? Put away your wine from you." Hannah answered and said, "No, my lord; I am a woman of a sorrowful spirit. I have drunk neither wine nor strong drink, but I have poured out my soul before the Lord. Count not your handmaid for a daughter of Belial; for out of the abundance of my complaint and grief have I spoken.' Then Eli answered and said, 'Go in peace; and the God of Israel grant you your petition that you have asked of Him.' And she said, 'Let Your handmaid find grace in your sight.' So the woman went her way, ate, and her countenance was no longer sad."

I have taken the time to type out the above passage so that we can pick out some verses and discuss them. According to verse 5, Hannah received a worthy portion whenever they went up to Shiloh to worship and sacrifice to the Lord. She got the worthy portion because Elkanah wanted to please Hannah, whom he loved, even though the Lord had shut her womb. According to verses 6 and 7, Hannah endured additional pain from Peninnah's provocation year after year; Hannah wept and did not eat. What a time of pain she went through! From verses 9 to 14, Hannah made up her mind to elevate her prayer life. She was so determined that her fervent prayer made Eli, the priest, think she was drunk, and he spoke roughly to her. In verses 15 and 16, we see her humility in answering Eli. In verses 17 and 18, Eli the priest told her, "Your petition is granted." Oh, hallelujah! She went home and ate.

Lessons from Hannah:
1. She was a woman of strong faith.

2. She understood that the Lord had closed her womb. Her adversary took advantage of this to provoke her.
3. She did not confront Peninnah, nor was she angry with her husband.
4. She could reach an impasse in her life and fall completely due to her pain, especially since she received no response from the Lord.
5. We observe her faith and focus on the Lord. In verses 10 and 11, in deep anguish, she prayed to the Lord and wept bitterly. In her pain, she found comfort and made a vow to the Lord.
6. Hannah needed a child, and the Lord needed a Prophet.

Beloved, I don't know what you have been through for many years—

whether concerning your own life, children, or grandchildren. It doesn't matter how long the enemy has mocked you, asking, "Where is your God?" Listen, there is an expiration date.

Jeremiah 32:27: "Behold, I am the Lord God of all flesh: Is there anything too hard for Me?"

He sees those tears!

THE SECOND BIBLICAL EXAMPLE: THE WOMAN OF CANAAN
(Matthew 15:21-28)

"Then Jesus departed from there and went into the region of Tyre and Sidon. And behold, a woman of Canaan came out from that same

region and cried out to Him, saying, 'Have mercy on me, O Lord, Son of David; my daughter is severely demon-possessed.' But He answered her not a word. His disciples came and urged Him, saying, 'Send her away, for she cries out after us.' But He answered and said, 'I was not sent except to the lost sheep of the house of Israel.' Then she came and worshiped Him, saying, 'Lord, help me.' But He answered and said, 'It is not good to take the children's bread and throw it to the dogs.' She said, 'Yes, Lord, yet even the dogs eat the crumbs which fall from their master's table.' Then Jesus answered and said to her, 'O woman, great is your faith! Let it be to you as you desire.' And her daughter was healed from that very hour."

This woman's daughter was suffering from a serious demonic attack. Being a Canaanite, she must have heard about the Lord Jesus, a man who went about doing good by healing and delivering the demon-possessed. She also knew that Jesus was a Jew and that Jews had nothing in common with the Gentiles, but that didn't deter her. She found Jesus at the coast of Tyre and Sidon, leaving her daughter at home. It is unclear whether she intended to leave her daughter behind or not, but the Bible clearly states that she approached Jesus without her.

This woman was incredibly determined. I believe that the Lord Jesus had already seen or heard of this woman before coming to that coast. Just after He helped her, as indicated in verse 29, He moved on. The Lord hears your cry! According to verses 22-26, she faced hurtful responses from the Lord's disciples and Jesus Himself. One might think she would become discouraged at this point, but she was so determined not to take no for an answer. In verse 27, she touched the Lord's heart with her humility, and in verse 28, He said, "O woman, great is your faith! Let it be to you as you desire." Her daughter was made whole from that very hour. The key point here is that she made up her mind to push through the storm of hurtful words by having faith in the Lord Jesus, and as a result, she received her solution.

Lessons from the Canaanite Woman:
1) She must have heard about the Lord Jesus before, and also that He was a Jew, and that Jews and Gentiles had nothing in common.
2) She had an extraordinary faith to believe that she would receive a miracle from the Lord.
3) From all indications we can tell she had been crying out and looking forward to the day she would meet with the Lord.
4) We can also remark that the Lord heard her cry before coming to the coast of

Tyre and Sidon because that was the only case that He handled.

5) She was humble and determined.

Do you have a problem? Yours might not be like hers. Don't allow the voice of the enemy or any negative voice to discourage you or talk you down. Focus on the Lord and be determined to endure. Remember, the Lord sees those tears shed in secret places. Even in your wilderness, the Lord will open your eyes to see a well (Genesis 21:17). Also remember that the enemy will not celebrate you for starting to pray; he will try to make you feel that your case is hopeless.

THE THIRD BIBLICAL EXAMPLE: THE WOMAN WITH THE ISSUE OF BLOOD
(Mark 5:25-34)

"And a certain woman had a flow of blood for twelve years, and had suffered many things from many physicians. She had spent all that she had and was no better but rather grew worse. When she heard about Jesus, she came from behind in the crowd and touched His garment. For she said, "If only I may touch His clothes, I shall be made whole." Immediately, the fountain of her blood was dried up, and she felt in her body that she was healed of that affliction.

And Jesus, immediately knowing in Himself that power had gone out of

Him, turned around in the crowd and said, 'Who touched my clothes?'" His disciples said to Him, "You see the multitude thronging You, and You say, 'Who touched Me?'"

Others were around, merely to press against Jesus, but this woman came with determination, and she received what she sought.

"He looked around to see her who had done this thing. But the woman, fearing and trembling, knowing what had happened to her, came and fell down before Him and told Him the whole truth. And He said to her, 'Daughter, your faith has made you

whole. Go in peace and be healed of your affliction."'

Verse 26 mentions that she suffered MANY things at the hands of MANY physicians; "I don't know how MANY is MANY." She spent all that she had, and the situation only worsened after bleeding for 12 years. Lord, have mercy!

Lessons from the Woman with the Issue of Blood:

1) She was a woman of extraordinary faith.
2) She knew that due to her condition, she was not supposed to be in the midst of people. She had this condition for 12 years.
3) Verse 26 says that she suffered many things, from many physicians, and even

spent everything she had, but her condition grew worse. At that point, she could give up but she didn't.

4) When she heard about the Lord Jesus, she made up her mind in her condition to see if she could touch just the hem of this Holy Man's garments.

5) At that time it was like do or die! The enemy must have tried to talk her down, saying: "Remember you are unclean" but she tore the line and got her miracle.

Beloved child, man, woman of God, I don't know what you are going through right now. Is it about your family, health, or finances? The Lord Jesus is the way, the truth, and the life. He has promised, He will never leave us nor forsake us

(Hebrews 13:5). That woman was just a woman like you and me. Twelve years was not twelve days. She persevered under longsuffering, took her faith to another level, and got her miracle.

THE FOURTH BIBLICAL EXAMPLE: MARY MAGDALENE
(Luke 7:37-39)

The first encounter of Mary Magdalene with the Lord Jesus:

> *"One of the pharisees asked Jesus to have dinner with him, so Jesus went to his home and sat down to eat. When a certain immoral woman from that city heard He was eating there, she brought a beautiful alabaster jar*

filled with expensive perfume. Then knelt behind Him at His feet, weeping. Her tears fell on His feet, and she wiped them off with her hair. Then she kept kissing His feet and putting perfume on them. When the Pharisee who had invited Him saw this, he said to himself, 'If this man were a Prophet, he would know what kind of woman is touching him. She is a sinner'" (Luke 7:37-39, NLT.)

Mary Magdalene had a Spiritual problem; she was known as a notorious sinner in her community. Whenever anyone in her community saw her, they would say, "That's a sinner!" That may explain why the man who invited Jesus for dinner doubted if Jesus were a Prophet. If Jesus were a

Prophet, he would have known that the woman was a sinner and shouldn't have allowed her to touch him. There are people in our communities today who are captives in the hands of the enemy, and there is no one willing to help, because to them, they have nothing to do with a sinner.

Jesus came to set the captives free (Luke 4:18-19). Mary Magdalene took a bold step and entered the house of a Pharisee to meet Jesus. We are not for told how long she had been in that captivity, but when she heard about Jesus, approached Him with faith and determination to receive her deliverance, and she was set free. After her deliverance, she followed the Lord, and was among other women who ministered to the Lord with their substances (Luke 8:2-3). In

Mathew 27:61, it is written that Mary Magdalene and one other woman sat right across the sepulcher where the Lord was buried.

In John 20:1, it is recorded that on the first day of week, while it was yet dark, Mary Magdalene came to the Tomb of Jesus with spices, which she had prepared and put them on the dead body of Jesus. When she arrived at the sepulcher, she could not find the body of Jesus, so she ran back to tell Peter and John, who followed her, and found the Tomb empty.

John 20:10-18: "Then the Disciples went away to their own home. But Mary stood without at the sepulcher weeping: and as she wept, she stooped down, and looked into the sepulcher, and seeth two angels in white sitting, the one at the head, and the other at feet, where the body of Jesus had lain. And they asked her, woman, why weepest thou? And she said unto them, because they have taken away my Lord, and I know not where they have laid him. And when she has thus said, she turned herself back, and saw Jesus standing, and knew not that he was Jesus.

Jesus saith unto her, "Woman, why weepest thou? Whom seekest thou?" She supposing him to be the gardener, said unto him, "Sir, if thou has borne him hence, tell me where thou hast laid him, and I will take him away."

Jesus saith unto her, "Mary". She turned herself, and saith unto Him, "Rabboni"; which is to say Master.

Jesus saith unto her, "Touch me not; for I am not yet ascended to My Father, and your Father; and to My God, and your God."

Mary Magdalene came and told the disciples that she has seen the Lord, and that He had spoken these things unto her."

This is Hard, But True: The Lord will Test Our Perseverance:

1) He saw Mary when she left her house with determination to come to the Tomb while it was yet dark.

2) He saw when she ran back to tell Peter and John.
3) He saw how she was courageous; when she was left alone by the disciples at the Tomb.
4) The Lord was not moved.
5) Mary was looking for a corpse, not angels, or Guard.

The woman who stopped the Lord Jesus from going to the Father first received these words from the risen Lord: "TOUCH ME NOT; FOR I AM NOT YET ASCENDED TO MY FATHER: BUT GO TO MY BRETHREN, AND SAY UNTO THEM, I ASCEND UNTO MY FATHER, AND YOUR FATHER, AND TO MY GOD, YOUR GOD."

Lessons from the Mary Magdalene:

1) She was the first to see the risen Lord.
2) She was known in her community as a notorious sinner.

I don't know what you are known for in your community; the ugly names the enemy has given you, to turn you unto destruction don't matter! You can make a U-turn! Take hold of the feet of Jesus and He will change your story.

I put prayer topics, and some scriptures at the end of each topic, so that you can read the scriptures, and take time to pray the topics. Remember that this is a prayer guide. Don't just read through the topics, and say amen at the end. You can use this guide to lead your prayer groups during your prayer meetings:

PRAYER TOPICS

1. *Father, thank You for Your loving-kindness for me and my family. Psalm 118:1*
2. *Father, I thank You because my breath is in Your hands.*
3. *Father thank You for translating me from the kingdom of darkness into the Kingdom of your dear Son. Colossians 1:13-14.*
4. *Thank You Lord for the life stories of Hannah and other women in Scripture; You have opened my eyes to see the determination of women like me.*
5. *Lord, baptize me with the Holy Ghost and fire. Matthew 3:11.*
6. *Dear Holy Spirit, baptize me with the fire of faith.*

7. *Dear Lord, baptize me with the fire of persistent prayer, and intercession. Luke 18:1-8.*

8. *Dear Holy Spirit, teach me how to pray without ceasing. I Thessalonians 5:17.*

9. *Dear Holy Spirit, give me the grace to elevate my prayer life to another dimension, to be determined and persevere without giving up, until I receive my petition, in the name of Jesus.*

10. *I command any network of stagnation against my life to be broken into pieces, in the name of Jesus. Isaiah 8:9.*

11. *Let every evil counsel against my life come to naught, in the name of Jesus. Isaiah 8:10.*

12. *Lord Jesus, do not spew me out of Your mouth. Revelation 3:15-16.*

13. *Dear Holy Spirit, teach me how to buy gold refined by fire. Revelation 3:17-18.*
14. *Dear Holy Spirit, help me to return to my first love. Revelation 2:4-5.*
15. *Father, cause my rod to bud. Numbers 17:6-8.*
16. *Dear Holy Spirit, give grace to persevere and not give up. Luke 18:1-8.*

Add your own topics.

Please, spend time to pray with those you are leading to pray using this prayer guide.

Prayer is the major weapon of every believer in Christ.

Chapter Three

A WOMAN IS A VESSEL IN THE HANDS OF THE LORD

THE FIRST EXAMPLE: VIRGIN MARY

Luke 1:27-33: "To a virgin espoused to a man whose name was Joseph, of the house of David; and the virgin's name was Mary. And the angel came unto her and said, 'Hail, thou that art highly favored, the Lord is with thee;

blessed art thou among women.' And when she saw him, she was troubled at his saying, and cast in her mind what manner of salutation this should be. And the angel said unto her, 'Fear not, Mary: for thou hast found favor with God. And behold, thou shalt conceive in thy womb and bring forth a son, and shall call his name Jesus. He shall be great and shall be called the Son of the Highest: and the Lord God shall give unto him the throne of his father David.'"

The Virgin Mary was engaged to a fiancé named Joseph, but unknown to her, the Lord had an assignment for her to carry out before she got married. What was this assignment? The angel told her that she would give birth to the ONE Whose Kingdom will last forever. What an embarrassment it must have been for her! What was she going to tell her fiancé? Nevertheless, by faith, she accepted and yielded herself to the Lord's will. The Lord used her to fulfill His Word in Genesis 3:15. Women, you are vessels in the hands of the Lord!

THE SECOND EXAMPLE: DEBORAH

In Judges 4:4, we see that Deborah was a prophetess and also served as a judge over Israel at that time. According to verses 6-7, the Lord used her as a prophetess to give directions to Barak, who was a military commander and judge. Yet,

Barak could not face Sisera, the captain of Canaan, without her by his side (Judges 4:8-9). Judges 5:7 refers to Deborah as a mother in Israel. The Lord used her as a vessel to conquer Sisera and his army through Barak. That was a woman just like you and me.

Dear Holy Spirit, help us in our dispensation!

THE THIRD EXAMPLE:
ANNA THE WIDOW

Luke 2:36-38: "And there was one Anna, the prophetess, the daughter of Phanuel of the tribe Asher: she was of a great age, and lived with an husband seven years from her virginity; And she was a widow of about fourscore, and four years [that is 84 years]; which departeth not from the temple, but served God with fastings and prayers night and day. [O Lord!!!] And she coming in that instant gave thanks likewise unto the Lord, and spake of Him to all them that looked for redemption in Jerusalem."

Can you imagine a woman of that age serving God with fasting, and prayers night and day, not departing from the Temple?

Anna was married for seven years, but nothing was said about her having children during that time. After becoming a widow, she could remarry because she was still young. However, she remained devoted to the Lord, praying and fasting for those seeking redemption in Jerusalem. Sisters, can we take such a risk to pray for our own families? O Lord!

THE FOURTH EXAMPLE: QUEEN ESTHER

Esther, unknown to her, was an orphan—both parents gone—but her uncle Mordecai was placed in her life by the Lord for His plans, which were also unknown to Mordecai. He took care of her both physically and spiritually. Is the Lord placing on your heart to care for an orphan? Act quickly; you never know what that child may become tomorrow.

Let me share a story about a mistreated orphan I saw in my village. A woman married a man who had lost his first wife, and he had a child from that marriage. When she began bearing her own children, she treated the orphan cruelly. The child cried out, and the Lord heard her cry, following His word in Exodus 22:22-24. We must be careful about how we treat orphans.

Back to Esther's story; the story is a bit long, but I'll get straight to the important part. She became the Queen of Persia after the former queen disobeyed the king (Esther 1:12), and her uncle Mordecai was one of the gatekeepers. The king promoted Haman above all the princes, and there was trouble because Mordecai refused to bow to him (Esther 3:1-5). Haman, enraged by Mordecai's defiance, sought to annihilate all the Jews, requiring a written decree from the king and offering to pay ten thousand talents of silver—around $3.48 billion—into the king's treasury, to execute this plan (Esther 3:8-9). In verses 10-11, the king accepted, and gave the go-ahead for the destruction of ALL the Jews in that land. News of the royal decree to destroy ALL the Jews spread throughout the Persian provinces, leading to mourning, fasting, and weeping among the Jewish people (Esther 4:1-3). "O Lord, may the Church arise to mourn, fast, weep, and wail against the evil orders impacting families and the Church!"

WHAT FASTING AND PRAYERS CAN DO

Queen Esther instructed the Jews through Mordecai (Esther 4:16):

> *"Go, gather together all the Jews who are present in Shushan, and fast for me; neither eat nor drink for three days. I and my maidens will fast likewise; and I will go to the king, which is against the law; and if I perish, I perish."*

This statement: "If I perish, I perish" underscores that even the queen recognized the gravity of her situation, and courageously stepped forward for her people; even she the Queen wasn't normally authorized to go in unto the king without his approval.

In Esther 5:1-3, it says that on the third day, Queen Esther put on her royal apparel and stood in the inner court of the king's house. She found favor in the king's eyes, and he asked her what her request was, ready to grant her even half of his kingdom. Can you imagine what three days of sincere prayer and fasting can do? From verses 3 to 8, we see that the king was not at ease. He even promised Esther half of his kingdom without knowing her request, showing just how eager he was to please her. All of this was a result of her three days of prayer and fasting. Esther was humble and wise enough to invite both the king and Haman to a banquet. She did this not just once, but twice—what a patient woman!

A Woman is a Vessel in the Hands of the Lord

Meanwhile, Haman was boasting to his wife and friends about being invited to dine with the queen and the king. Yet, he could not fully enjoy his happiness because he was bothered by Mordecai not bowing down to him. Even with two royal invitations, his joy was incomplete as he kept on thinking about Mordecai defiance against him. Listen to me, in this season as you take hold of the Feet of the Lord in prayers, your enemy will eat bread with tears in his eyes, in the mighty name of Jesus!

In verses 13-14, Haman's wife and friends advised him to build gallows to hang Mordecai. Hear me: because God's children do not make gallows for their enemies, whoever is preparing a gallows for you will be hanged on his or her own gallows, in the mighty name of Jesus.

Mordecai's Deeds Made Known

Esther 6:1 states,

> *"That night, the king could not sleep, so he commanded that the books of records of the chronicles, be brought to him."*

What caused the king to lose sleep that night? It was the sincere prayers of God's people.

Verse 2 reveals that it was found written that Mordecai had informed the king about Bigthana and Teresh, two of the king's chamberlains, who had sought to harm King Ahasuerus.

In verse 3, the king asked,

"What honor and dignity have been bestowed upon Mordecai for this?"

The king's servants answered,

"Nothing has been done for him."

Verses 4-12: "And the king said, who is in the court? Now Haman was come in to the outward court of the king's house, to speak unto the king to hang Mordecai on the gallows that he has prepared for him. And the king's servants said unto him, 'Behold, Haman standeth in the court.' And the king said, 'let him come in.' So Haman came in, and the king said unto to him, 'what shall be done unto the man whom the king delight to honour?'

Now Haman thought in his heart, 'To whom would the king delight to honour more than myself?' And Haman answered the king, 'For the man whom the king delights to honour, let the royal apparel be brought, which the king uses to wear, and the horse that the king rides upon, and the crown royal is set upon his head: and let this apparel and the horse be delivered to the hand of one of the king's most noble princes, that they array the man with whom the king delights to honour, and bring him on horseback through the street of the city, proclaiming before him, 'Thus shall it be done to the man whom the king delights to honour.

Then the king said to Haman, "Make haste, and take the apparel, and the horse, as thou hast said, and do even to Mordecai the Jew, that sits at the king's gate: let nothing fail of all that thou has spoken.'

Then took Haman the apparel, and the horse, and arranged Mordecai, and brought him on horseback through the street of the city, and proclaimed before him, 'Thus shall it be done unto the man whom the king delights to honour.' And Mordecai came again to the king's gate."

In this season, your enemy will be the one to describe how you will be honored, in the mighty name of Jesus! If someone had told Mordecai about this unexpected honor orchestrated through Haman, he would never have believed it. That is the power of prayer. I pray that the books of remembrance be opened for anyone praying with this message, in the name of Jesus!

> *Verse 12b: "But Haman hasted to his house mourning, and having his head covered, that's humiliated."*

Your enemy will eat bread with tears in his eyes!

Haman's Fall Predicted

When Haman told his wife, Zeresh, and all his friends everything that had befallen him, his wise men and Zeresh said to him, "If Mordecai is of the seed of the Jews, before whom you have begun to fall, you shall not prevail against him, but shall surely fall before him." While they were still talking with him, the king's chamberlains hastened to bring Haman to the banquet that Esther had prepared.

Esther's Banquet for the king and Haman

Esther 7:1-10: "So the king and Haman came to banquet with Esther the Queen. And the king said again unto Esther on the second day at the banquet of wine, 'what is thy petition, Queen Esther? and it shall be granted thee: and what is thy request? and it shall be performed, even to the half of the kingdom.'

Then Esther the queen answered and said, 'If I have found favour at thy sight, O king, and if it please the king, let my life be given me at my petition, and my people for my request. For we are sold, I and my people, to be destroyed, to be slain, and to perish. But if we have been sold for bondmen and bondwomen, I had held my tongue, although the enemy couldn't countervail the king's damage.'

Then the king Ahasuerus answered and said unto Esther the Queen, 'Who is he, and where is he, that durst presume in his heart to do so?' And Esther said, 'The adversary and enemy is this wicked Haman. Then

Haman was afraid before the king and the Queen.

Let's review what we have read from Esther chapters 4-7.

- In chapter 4:1, Mordecai did not wait after perceiving the enemy's plan; he cried with a loud bitter cry;
- In verse 3, the Jews in every province were mourning, fasting, weeping, and praying;
- In verse 16, Queen Esther sent for THREE DAYS OF FASTING AND PRAYERS, with no eating or drinking for all the Jews in Shushan. She and her maidens joined them, praying in one accord for her to find favor before the king;

- In Chapter 5:1-2, on the third day, she took a risk and entered the inner court of the king's house, and behold, she found favor before the king;
- In chapter 6:1, the records of the chronicles were opened;
- In verses 4-11, Haman was made to describe how Mordecai should be honored, and he was the one whom the king assigned to carry out the process.
- Verses 12-13: HAMAN'S FALL PREDICTED. A Jew, a child of God, is the apple of His eye: Psalm 17:8.
- FINALLY, in Chapter 7:6-10, the enemy was exposed and hanged on his own gallows.

Let's go back to Esther chapter 4:12-14:

"And they told to Mordecai, Esther's words. Then Mordecai commanded to answer Esther, 'Think not with thy self that thou Shall escape in the King's house, more than all the Jews. For if thou altogether holdest thy peace at this time, then shall there enlargement, and deliverance arise to the Jews from another place; but thou and thy father's house shall be destroyed: And who knoweth whether thou art come to kingdom for such a time as this?'"

"Who knows whether you have come to the kingdom for such a time as this?" Queen Esther came to herself after the above statement.

Queen Esther was just a woman like you and me. She humbled herself and was patient in giving her answer to the king, who was anxious to hear her request. Esther was not swayed by the king's promise to give her half of his kingdom. Her request was significant: "her life and those of her people." She patiently humbled herself and delivered her request to the king at the right moment.

Prayer Topics

Read the scriptures, and take time to pray.

1. *Holy One of Israel, we come in to Your presence with praise and thanksgiving, worshipping You our Creator. Revelation 4:11.*

2. Thank You Lord for the Biblical examples of vessels.
3. Father, I thank You because my breath is in Your hands.
4. Dear Holy Spirit, help me to depend on You, and be conscious of Your presence so that I do not grieve You. Ephesians 4:30.
5. We pray O Lord! Raise women in our generation who will position themselves through the power of the Holy Spirit for You to use as vessels. 2 Timothy 2:21.
6. Father, deliver me from nonchalant attitude in the name of Jesus. Isaiah 32:9-11.
7. Thank Lord for teaching my hands to war, and my fingers to fight, in the name of Jesus. Psalm 144:1.
8. I take authority to tear down yokes of ancestral foundations, against my life and

those of my descendants, in the Name of Jesus. Judges 6:25-27.

9. *We apply the blood of Jesus by the power of the Holy Spirit to proclaim better blessings for the children in the mighty name of Jesus.*
10. *Dear Holy Spirit, help me to pray for the Pastors, the Church, and the Nation. 1 Timothy 2:1-2.*

Add your own topics, as led by the Holy Spirit.

Chapter Four

PRAYER IS HARD WORK

NEHEMIAH REBUILDS
THE BROKEN WALL
(Nehemiah 4:1-3)

"But it came to pass, that when Samballat heard that we builded the wall, he was wroth, and filled with too great indignation, and mocked the Jews and spake before his brethren

> *and the army of Samaria, 'What do these feeble Jews? [in other words, what are these feeble Jews trying to do?] Will they fortify themselves? Will they make an end in a day? Will they revive the stones out of the heaps of rubbish which are burned?'*
>
> *Now Tobiah the Ammonite was by him, and he said, 'Even that which they build, if a fox go up, he shall even break down the stone wall.'"*

The story above is lengthy, but I want to make a point. From Chapter 1 of the book of Nehemiah, we see that Nehemiah heard about the broken wall of Jerusalem, and he was deeply affected by this bad news. He began to pray with fasting and repentance. It took him some time and effort in prayer to find favor with the king he was serving, in order to be allowed to go to Jerusalem and figure out how to rebuild the city's walls. It was hard work, requiring prayer and fasting. But here, the enemy referred to them as feeble. The enemy did not applaud their efforts to rebuild the walls; instead, they were mocked and ridiculed.

When you decide to rebuild the lives of your children and families through fasting and prayer, do not expect the enemy to celebrate your efforts. He will wait patiently to see how far you can go, and when you persist, he will attempt to discourage you with distractions, tiredness, and doubts. But you must remain determined to persevere. In the scripture above, Nehemiah did not respond to the enemy's taunts; instead, he and his men turned to the Lord in prayer (Nehemiah 4:4-6). Remember, the enemy comes to kill; he does not come to play with you. He wanted Nehemiah and his people to feel discouraged and to believe that if a fox were to climb their stone walls, they would collapse.

DAVID BEFORE GOLIATH
(1 Samuel 17:44)

"The Philistine said to David, 'Come to me, and I will give thy flesh unto the bowls of the air, and the beast of the fields.'"

When David first saw this soldier, who had fought in conflicts for many years, one may assume that he would give up, but let's hear what he had to say instead in verses 45-47:

> *"Then said David to the Philippine, 'Thou cometh to me with a sword, and with a spear, and with a shield: but I come to thee in the name of the Lord of Hosts, the God of the Armies of Israel, Whom thou has defied. This day will the Lord deliver thee into mine hand; and I will smite thee, and take thine head from thee, and I will give the carcases of the host of the Philippines this day unto the fowls of the air, and to the wild beasts of the Earth; that all the earth may know that there is a God in Israel. And all this assembly shall know that the Lord saveth not with*

sword and spear: for the battle is the Lord's, and He will give you into our hands."'

What a declaration of a shepherd boy? But he trusted with all confidence that The Lord will give the enemy into his hands. At last, David had to cut off the head of Goliath. Verse (51). Rise up women of fire, and cut off the head of the enemy that has been intimidating you all these years. Be strong in The Lord, and the power of His might; put on your spiritual Armor.

IS YOUR CASE LIKE THE DRY BONES?
(Ezekiel 37:1-3)

"The Hand of The Lord was on Ezekiel, and took him in to a valley

which was full of bones, and the bones were VERY DRY. The Lord asked Ezekiel, 'Son of man, can these bones live? [In other words, is it possible for these VERY DRY BONES to live?] And He answered, 'O Lord God Thou knowest.'"

In verse 4, the Lord instructed Ezekiel to prophesy to the dry bones, telling them to hear the Word of the Lord—not Ezekiel's own words.

In verses 5 and 6, the Lord revealed to Ezekiel what he should say to the dry bones.

In verse 7, Ezekiel prophesied as he was commanded. There was a shaking as he obeyed the Lord and spoke the Word of the Lord to the dry bones. It is important to note that the Lord could have brought the bones to life on His own, but He chose to partner with Ezekiel. The Lord is ready to cause the dry bones in your family to live, but you must prophesy and obey His Word.

THIS IS YOUR GENERATION!
(Psalm 139:16)

"Thine eyes did see my substance, yet being unperfect; and in Thy book all my members were written, which in continuance were fashioned, when as yet there was none of them."

The Lord saw our complete beings long before we were formed in our mothers' wombs. Everything about us, including our purposes for being created and those of our descendants, is written in

His book. If you have been born again—meaning you have realized that you were just following your parents to church, but then came to a point where you confessed your sins to the Lord and asked Him to be your personal Lord and Savior—now you can, through prayer, ask the Holy Spirit to reveal your purpose for creation to you. You may also seek guidance from a pastor or a mature person in the Lord. But remember, you were not created or born to live your life just the way you want; the Lord formed you in the womb for a purpose.

PRAYER IS WORK!

Women, the Lord Jesus is calling us to rise up and break those evil foundations that have stood against our destinies and those of our descendants.

> *Exodus 20:1-6: "And God spake all these words, saying, 'I am the Lord thy God, which have brought thee out of the land of Egypt, and out of the house of bondage. Thou shalt have no other gods before me. Thou shalt not make unto thee any graven image, or any likeness of anything that is in heaven above, or that is in the earth beneath, or that is in the water under the earth. Thou shalt not bow thyself to them, nor serve them: for I, the Lord thy God, am a jealous God, visiting the iniquity of the fathers upon the children unto the third and fourth generation of them*

that hate me; and showing mercy unto thousands of them that love me and keep my commandments."

We all come from different backgrounds. Some of us used to follow our grandparents and parents in worshipping idols until the Lord, through the power of the Holy Spirit, opened our understanding to accept the Lord Jesus into our lives as our personal Lord and Savior—the only One we should bow to.

CALLED TO STAND IN THE GAP FOR YOUR FAMILIES

Do not blame anyone who is CHAINED in idol worship or DRUG addiction, you name it. Remember that there is a force keeping them bound, and it will take the kind of prayers continuously offered by the Church, for the Lord to send an angel to release those in bondage, just as He did for Apostle Peter. The Church's determination to pray in the house of a woman named Mary, the mother of John Mark, showed great resolve (Acts 12:12). I don't know why this prayer was made in the house of a woman. Prayer is work; the Bible states that *"prayer was made without ceasing."*

It doesn't matter how deep and how long the destinies of our descendants have been buried in rubbish, in dungeons, and the like; we will stand on the finished work of the Cross to call them forth.

THE BLOOD OF JESUS SPEAKS BETTER THINGS

Let's consider Exodus 12:1-28. While I won't type out all of it, I will highlight some verses to illustrate that although the blood mentioned was from a one-year-old lamb (verse 5), it served as a covering.

Verse 7, "And they shall take of the blood, and strike it on the two side posts and on the upper door post of the houses, wherein they shall eat it."

Verse 23, "For the Lord will pass through to smite the Egyptians; and when He sees the blood upon the lintel and on the two side posts, the Lord will pass over the door, and will not suffer the destroyer to come in unto your houses to smite you."

This account refers to Moses and the Children of Israel as they prepared to leave Egypt.

That was just one little thing I picked out of so many that the Old Testament has concerning the blood.

Now let's jump to the New Testament:

Hebrews 12:24: "And to Jesus the mediator of the new covenant, and to the blood of sprinkling, that speaks better things than that of Abel."

There are many better things that the Blood of Jesus speaks, but you have to ask Him for His Blood, through the revelation of the Holy Spirit, to speak those better things on your behalf and on behalf of your family members.

To name a few examples: In Exodus 12:23, the blood served as a covering for the Israelites in the Old Testament. That blood pointed to the Precious Blood of the Lamb of God, the Lord Jesus, who paid for our salvation.

Just as I apply the authority given to me in Luke 10:19, I also apply the Precious Blood of Jesus to speak better things for me. Whatever better things I need, it is up to me to ask. The Power in the Blood of Jesus is immense. There is much to say about the power of the Blood of Jesus, as the songwriter said, "There is power, power, wonder-working power in the

Blood of the Lamb," reflecting his own experiences.

You can only truly understand the power of the Blood of Jesus when you apply it to speak better things on your behalf. I don't know how many better things you need; that's up to you. I have many experiences with the Blood of Jesus, as I have called upon His Blood to advocate for me. Let me share just one of those experiences:

One day, I had a dream where I found myself caged in a large, fenced area, with a high iron gate as the entrance. As I looked around, terrified and uncertain of how I would escape, I suddenly heard the Holy Spirit prompt me to say, "The Blood of Jesus." As I repeated this three times, I found myself standing right next to the massive gate, and astonishingly, it opened on its own. There was no one else around; I only saw the terrifying fence.

It is one thing to know that there is power in the Blood of Jesus, but it is another thing altogether to apply His blood to speak for you. Are you in trouble or in need of help? Ask the Holy Spirit to teach you more about the power in the Blood of Jesus and how to utilize that power.

GO FOR ANOINTING!

In 2019, I was leading the Intercessors at the ARC. We gathered for prayer every Friday night from 11 pm to 2 am. One Friday, as I prepared for the night's prayer,

I lay down to rest in the prayer room. It was a large space, with seats on both the right and left sides. Suddenly, I fell into a trance and saw the Intercessors sitting on either side of the room. To my right, I noticed a significant amount of oil dripping from the ceiling. While still in the trance, I stretched out my right hand to collect the oil and asked someone to provide me with a container. One of the sisters, Wanda Smith, pulled out a gallon from underneath her seat. However, before she could hand it to me, the Intercessors on my left side became unified and rushed over to collect the oil. At that moment, I felt the urgency to have a container available so I could distribute the oil for everyone to touch, but I ended up not taking the gallon. Shockingly, those on my right side, where the oil was pouring down, were not moved at all.

The following day, The next day, I sought the Lord's guidance to understand the meaning of the trance.. The Holy Spirit specifically revealed to me that the oil symbolizes anointing, and that individuals must seek the anointing for themselves; one cannot collect it to share with others. I pray that we will position ourselves to pray and ask the Lord to anoint us so that we can fulfill the purposes for which we were created.

"Dear lovely Holy Spirit, our Teacher, Helper, and Comforter, come! We cannot do without You." Ask the Holy Spirit to baptize you with the FIRE of intercession.

PRAYER TOPICS

1. *Father thank You for Your loving-kindness upon my life. Psalm 117:1.*
2. *Holy One of Israel, I worship You for my breath is in Your hands. Job 12:10.*
3. *Thank You Lord for choosing me to intercede. Isaiah 32:9.*
4. *Dear Holy Spirit, empower me to pray. Isaiah 62:6-7.*
5. *I decree and declare that every entanglement of the enemy against my descendants is broken in the name of Jesus. Isaiah 10:27.*
6. *Any stronghold of the enemy against the local Church to hinder the move of God, be blinded in the name of Jesus. Acts 13:6-12.*
7. *I command any network of the enemy from the pit of hell that is against the families, the Church, and the Nation to collide with the*

Dunamis power that is in the Name of Jesus. Philippians 2:10-11.

8. *Dear Holy Spirit, help me to use my spiritual arrows nonstop, in the name of Jesus. 2 Kings 13:14-19.*

9. *Let the enemies against my nation be judged at the borders in the name of Jesus. Ezekiel 11:10.*

10. *O Lord, the Supreme Commander of the Heavenly Armies, send us help! Joshua 5:13-15.*

11. *Father, I hold onto You to change the story of my family, the Church, and the nation, in the name of Jesus. Genesis 32:24-28.*

12. *Father, teach us to seek You and find You. Jeremiah 29:13.*

13. *Dear Holy Spirit, teach me the mystery of the four lepers. 2 Kings 7:3-7.*

You are called to pray while you read this prayer guide. Add your own prayer topics. This little book will help you to stand up as an army!

Conclusion

The Lord spoke to the daughters of Jerusalem, as we see in Luke 23:27-29, at the beginning of the first chapter of this book. He urged them "to pray for themselves" and then for their children. At this moment, He was on His way to be crucified, still preaching and warning.

The songwriter Isaac Watts wrote the hymn titled "When I Survey the Wondrous Cross," which reflects on the cross on which the Prince of Glory died. In the first stanza, he writes:

"When I survey the wondrous cross
On which the Prince of Glory died,
My richest gain I count but loss,
And pour contempt on all my pride."

I will only dwell on this first stanza. The hymn speaks of the wondrous, fantastic, and marvelous cross where the Lord was hung on three nails. His back was torn like chopped meat, and blood oozed from His head due to the crown of thorns. He could not wipe it away because His hands were nailed to the cross. His feet were nailed together with one long nail. Can you imagine His weight hanging on those three nails? Luke 23:34 records that even through the pain and blood, the Lord Jesus lifted His eyes to His Father and asked Him to forgive those who crucified Him. Do you have

CONCLUSION

someone in your life that you find difficult to forgive? You might justify this by thinking, "No one knows what this person did to me." However, you can take a lesson from our Lord and Savior, who, despite being in excruciating pain, still forgave.

Isaac Watts remarked that his richest gains were counted as loss, which reminds me of Apostle Paul in Philippians 3:7-8:

> *"But what things were gain to me, those I counted loss for Christ. Yea doubtless, and I count all things but loss for the excellency of the knowledge of Christ Jesus my Lord: for whom I have suffered the loss of all things, and do count them but dung, that I may win Christ."*

The last line of the first stanza of the hymn, "and pour contempt on all my pride", signifies a rejection of all disrespectful behavior.

Women of God, we live in a time where the enemy seeks to prevent us from praying. However, the Lord instructs us to pray for ourselves first and then for our children. May the Holy Spirit open our eyes to identify the hindrances in our lives that prevent us from praying, but I must tell you that the Holy Spirit can only help us in the place of prayer. Apostle Paul writes in Philippians 2:12:

"Therefore, my beloved, as you have always obeyed, not only in my presence but now much more in my

absence, work out your own salvation with fear and trembling."

Salvation is free, but it is not cheap!

In Luke 13:24, the Lord Jesus says:

"Strive to enter through the narrow gate; for many, I say to you, will seek to enter and will not be able."

Lord have mercy!

PRAYER TOPICS

1. *Holy One of Israel, I thank You for Your loving-kindness, and mercies that endure for me. Psalm 136:1.*

2. *Dear Holy Spirit, without you, I can do nothing. John 16:13-14.*

3. *Dear Holy Spirit, teach me to survey the Cross on which my price of Redemption was paid. Luke 9:28-31, 22:44.*

4. *O Lord, help me to run this race to the end. 1 Corinthians 9:24-26.*

5. *Dear Holy Spirit stir me up, open my eyes to differentiate the truth from the false. Matthew 24:3-4; 11-12, 2 Thessalonians 2:1-3.*

6. *Lord, help me to build an altar of fasting. Luke 2:36-37.*

7. *Help me Lord, to build on the Rock. Mathew 7:24-25.*

8. *Father, help me to pray fervently. James 5:16.*

9. *I bind any strong man fighting my prayer life, in the name of Jesus. Daniel 6:11-13.*

10. *O Lord arise and fight against the enemies assigned against the families, the Church, and the Nation. Numbers 16:28-33.*

CONCLUSION

I advise anyone praying with this prayer guide to read the scriptures at the end of the topics, and really take time to pray each topic. Don't just read through the topics.

For more information, please write to:
Mrs. Helen Wialo Chongsi
513 Brinwood Way
Oakley, CA 94561-3089
Email: helenchongsi11@gmail.com
Phone: (+1) 925-567-4167
(+237) 696-524-859
(+237) 677-21-97-22

Personal Notes

Made in the USA
Las Vegas, NV
14 February 2025